Charles Dewey Day

In the matter of the claim of the Hudson's Bay Company

closing argument of the claimants, in reply to the responsive argument for

the United States

Charles Dewey Day

In the matter of the claim of the Hudson's Bay Company
*closing argument of the claimants, in reply to the responsive argument for the
United States*

ISBN/EAN: 9783744740074

Printed in Europe, USA, Canada, Australia, Japan

Cover: Foto ©ninafisch / pixelio.de

More available books at **www.hansebooks.com**

BRITISH AND AMERICAN JOINT COMMISSION,

FOR

THE SETTLEMENT OF THE CLAIMS

OF THE

HUDSON'S BAY & PUGET'S SOUND AGRICULTURAL COMPANIES.

IN THE MATTER OF THE CLAIM

OF THE

HUDSON'S BAY COMPANY,

CLOSING ARGUMENT OF THE CLAIMANTS,

IN REPLY TO THE

RESPONSIVE ARGUMENT FOR THE UNITED STATES.

———◆•◆•◆———

Montreal:

PRINTED BY JOHN LOVELL, ST. NICHOLAS STREET.

1869.

CLAIM OF THE HUDSON'S BAY COMPANY.

CLOSING ARGUMENT OF THE CLAIMANTS.

To THE HONORABLE THE COMMISSIONERS.

In entering upon the task of replying to the Responsive argument produced in behalf of the United States, I propose to confine myself within very brief limits ; relying upon the fuller treatment of most of the subjects in the opening argument. If however in the endeavour thus to avoid repetition and prolixity, any points should be neglected upon which the Commissioners think that a more extended discussion is desirable, I shall of course hold myself in readiness at all times to conform to their requirements.

The answer of the Respondents to the opening argument in this case rests for the most part upon the assumptions which originated with Governor Stevens, and are embodied in his prejudiced report of 1853. Often as the pretensions set up in that pioneer document have been presented, so often have they been shewn to be unfounded and preposterous. They are again reproduced in the present argument, varied and exaggerated, but substantially the same.

I take up the paragraphs in the order in which I find them. The first is under the heading.

(A.)—GENERAL CONSIDERATIONS. (p. 3).

The proposition first announced here is that the expression " future appropriation " in the 3rd Art. of the Treaty of 1846, means one or both of two things. "1 *Taking* " (*by the United States*) "*for its own use such portions of land as it would need* "*for public purposes as military reservations, light houses, &c.;*" and " 2 *Establishing its land system over the Territory.*"—This is certainly an original if not very ingenious distortion of the meaning of a phrase so plain that one would suppose it could not be misunderstood. The language of the article is, that " in the future

" appropriation of the territory south of the 49th parallel of north
" latitude, *as provided in article I* of the said treaty, the possessory
" rights of the Hudson's Bay Company, and of all British subjects
" who may be already in the occupation of land or other property
" lawfully acquired within the said territory, shall be respected."
On turning to article I. of the Treaty we find there, the definition
of the boundary line which for the future was to separate the territories of the two Countries, and " the future appropriation of the
territory south of the 49th parallel of north latitude, *as provided in
article 1*," is without doubt, the appropriation to the United States
thenceforth, resulting from the Division then made.   The Counsel
for the United States felt this, and in quoting the article discreetly
omitted the words, *as provided in the first article* of the Treaty :
but with the restoration of the displaced words, the error of his
interpretation becomes apparent.   I am unwilling to reason upon
the pretensions of the Respondents in any other view of the meaning
of article 3, because it seems to me certain that it can mean nothing
else ; and if this opinion needed confirmation it would be found
in the language of the preamble of the Treaty, with which it perfectly harmonizes. (See preamble of Treaty of 1846, and also p. 22
of opening argument.) But even, if for the sake of argument, it were
admitted that the words " future appropriation " have the improbable
meaning contended for, it does not change the position of the Claimants.   The obligation would still be that the United States in ap-
propriating the territory of which it then first acquired the absolute
sovereignty and ownership, should respect the possessory rights of
the Hudson's Bay Company in it.   Anything more unreasonable and
untenable in either interpretation of the article than the assumptions
under numbers 1. 2. of this (A.) I. proposition, it would be difficult
to present.

II. p. 4. 5.   The question examined by the Respondents under
this division is, " What is the meaning of the term ' possessory rights'
as used in the treaty," and the propositions advanced upon it are :
     1st. that there is a distinction between *possessory* and *proprietary*
rights.
     2nd. That " possessory rights, are precisely the same thing as
rights of possession."

3rd. That " nothing can be possessed, but that which has actual physical substance," as a house, or a field, or a book—but that a right, which is incorporeal, cannot be possessed.

4th. That, as a consequence of the foregoing propositions, the possessory rights of the Company under the treaty are confined to land. I have not followed altogether the language or order of the Respondents' argument in stating the foregoing propositions, but have I believe given them fully and fairly. It will be seen from them, that all rights of trade and of navigation are excluded from the meaning of the term " possessory rights." For the purpose of avoiding repetition I now give passages in relation to these latter rights, from the pages 67 and 71 of the argument and shall in this connection partially advert to what is said on the subject under the heads, (C.) Right of Trade and (D.) Right of Navigation.

" Trade, says the argument p. 67 is not a thing of physical exist- " ence. It is impalpable, immaterial, ideal. It is not therefore " capable of actual possession in the sense which gives rise to " ' possessory rights.   *   *   *   *   We insist, then, that the guar- " anty of the treaty in regard to possessory rights does not apply to the trade of the Company.' " On p. 71, it is denied that the right of navigation is a possessory right.

It should be observed that under these two heads of trade and navigation, an entirely different course of argument, and one utterly irreconcileable with the foregoing passages, has been adopted; but this inconsistency will be briefly noticed hereafter.

I shall examine these four propositions in their order.

The Counsel begins his discussion under the present division, by a simple reference to the distinction between "*possessory* and *proprietary rights* " (p. 4), and then cautiously refrains from pushing this distinction into notice. But the truth is, he argues his case wholly as if the Hudson's Bay Company were obliged not only to prove possession but to prove title also, or such a possession as would amount in law to title. Now this was precisely what the words of the treaty were intended to prevent, and do prevent. If the words *proprietary rights* had been made use of in the treaty, this pretention would have been well founded, then the Company must have shewn title or possession equivalent to title; but both the high contracting parties well knew that under the circumstances of the country this was impossible, and hence the more liberal and comprehensive term *" possessory rights,"* was adopted, a term including all kinds of possession with their appurtenant rights, and making the *possideo quia possideo* a sufficient substitute for any other title. This is the plain common sense signification of the words in the Treaty, and it cannot be frittered away by any stretch of perverted ingenuity.

2. In order to give any show of support to the 3rd and 4th propositions stated above, the counsel for the Respondents has found it necessary to cast about for a new form of expression, and a new meaning, as a substitute for the words and meaning of the treaty, and he thinks he has found them in the words, " rights of possession." This he says is what " possessory rights " mean and this only was guaranteed. The distinction of meaning between the two forms of expression is somewhat shadowy and fine drawn, partaking of the extreme subtlety and hair splitting which run through the whole argument; but if the new words are intended to substitute for the meaning of the words " possessory rights," anything less than all the rights of whatever description actually possessed by the Claimants at the date of the treaty, they must be rejected as insufficient. The treaty without doubt guarantees the " rights of possession," but the guarantee also covers the possessions themselves and all rights of an appreciable character then actually held and exercised by the Company.

3.–4. The propositions 3 and 4 may be treated together. The assertion that nothing can be possessed which has not a physical existence, as a house, or a book, is only true in the very narrowest technical sense. But it is not true in any sense which makes it a possible test for defining the rights of the Claimants under the treaty. Even the possession of corporeal things is not necessarily an actual possession, it may be a symbolic one, and the latter is as effectual in law as the former ; but a symbolic possession will apply as well to rights as to corporeal things. To give one familiar example among many ; a debt not represented by any written title may be assigned. (I write under the civil law.) But the assignment does not of itself transfer possession to the assignee ; that is only given by a notice to the debtor, and, until such notice is given the title to the debt is in one party, and the possession of it in another. Here then is a symbolic delivery and possession of a right, which operates precisely like the manual delivery of a chattel.

The Commissioners do not need to be reminded that there are innumerable rights political and civil, some created by the law alone, others derived from the will or acts of individuals, which are not attached to any substance, or in the words of the argument, " do not grow out of that which has physical being : " *quæ sensu corporeo tangi non possunt, sed quæ in jure consistunt et intellectu tantum percipiuntur ;* and which, nevertheless, are held and enjoyed, sometimes by those to whom they justly belong, at others by intruders and wrong-doers : and such holding and enjoyment constitutes a well understood *possession of them*, as cognizable and appreciable, and as fully protected, by legal remedies as any possession of a physical substance. The civil law says, concerning this matter of possession, *jura non possidentur, sed quasi-possidentur*, and again, *non possidetur sed magis tenetur* ; nevertheless, the distinction was so little founded in the nature of things that the words *possidere, possessio* are constantly applied to rights as well by the sages of the Justinian Code themselves, as by the civilians after them. These distinctions are characterised by a great modern legist as the rigor of judicial expression ; and again, as mere pruderies of language ; and it is a quibble on words to say that the exercise and enjoyment of a right is not a possession of it.

But I feel that all this discussion is unnecessary, if not absolutely idle. No educated man can for a moment acquiesce in the absurd restrictions which the Respondents strive to impose upon the meaning of the word " possessory," to the exclusion of its broader and legitimate signification. It is a simple matter of definition. Possession is defined to be " anything valuable possessed, or enjoyed." Possessory is " having such possession." This is the full and complete signification of the word.

Now, that the right of carrying on a particular trade, the right of navigating a particular river, are substantial and appreciable rights, the use and exercise or (what is the same thing) the possession and enjoyment of which may be the subject of a guarantee in any international treaty, surely no man will deny, as a general proposition. The only question is, what language in a treaty will amount to such guarantee, and this question must be answered by the words themselves, aided by the circumstances under which they are used. Apply this to the present case. Look at the circumstances of the Claimants—their License of exclusive trade which the Respondents say in several parts of their argument were all they had in the country—look at the fact of their use and exercise of this trade—the large establishments for carrying it on—the great number of men employed—and the notoriety of its extent and activity—and how is it possible to affect a doubt in the face of all these interpretative circumstances, that this trade was included among the "possessory rights" guaranteed by the treaty. What possessory right could be more palpable, undeniable and appreciable, than this great and wide-spread trade. The same course of reasoning will apply to the navigation of the Columbia, and I therefore abstain from offering any special observation with respect to that right.

In fine, the proposition of the Respondents, that nothing can be possessed which has not a corporeal existence ; and that, consequently, the words "possessory rights," as used in the treaty, apply only to objects which can be seen and felt and handled, and therefore do not include the rights of trade and navigation, is of the narrowest technical character, and with the whole argument upon it, seems to me trivial and misplaced, in connection with the present investigation. I have dwelt upon it too long, for I have not the slightest apprehension that the Commissioners will, upon any grounds like these, arrive at the conclusion that rights of trade and of navigation cannot be possessed and therefore are not comprised within the guarantee assumed by the treaty.

III—p. 5. The next question discussed in the answer is : " What are the possessory rights of the Company to land." What follows from p. 5 to p. 7, Nos. 1, 2, 3, 4, with respect to the nature and extent of the possession, is fully answered in the Reply of the Puget Sound Agricultural Company, and in order to save the trouble of reference, I repeat the substance of what is said there, and in pretty nearly the same language.

It is undeniable that a concession was contained in the Treaty of 1846, that the Company had *possessory rights*. A similar concession is contained in the Treaty of 1863. It has been shown in the Argument in the Hudson's Bay Company's claim, (p. 22), that the former treaty was a compromise in which the United States Government assumed certain obligations in favor of the subjects of Great Britain. In Oregon, at that time there was no established law, and no paramount authority from which title could be derived. A grant from either State was forbidden by treaty; nobody owned or could own real estate otherwise than by that primary form of title, *possession*. That title was not only the highest, but the only one possible: and in protecting the rights of its subjects, the British Government adopted it as sufficient, as well before the Treaty as by it, and the United States Government admitted it by the latter to be so. It was a possession which both parties pretending to the right of sovereignty mutually consented by the Treaty, and Great Britain by many previous acts, should be regarded, as a title or as equivalent to a title. Nothing was then left to do, to establish title but to prove the fact of possession. The whole discussion concerning the difference between possessory rights and fee simple, is misapplied and barren. It is of no importance under the present claim, what legal technical name is given to the rights of the Claimants; if they are not a fee simple, they are a perpetual right of possession, and this is to be respected. A perpetual right of possession is equivalent in value to what the law calls a fee simple, and when it is relinquished, must be paid for according to its value, by whatever name it may be called.

Equally misapplied and useless is the discussion relating to Indian titles and preemption claims introduced here upon p. 7, and extended on pages numbered from 57 to 63.

The reference to the language of other treaties on p. 130 of the Responsive argument is sufficiently met by the observations contained in the Reply of the Puget Sound Agricultural Company, (p. 4–5).

But the great point upon which the whole argument of the Respondents is really based in this cause, is to be found under the number 5 upon p. 8, and the following pages to 14 and is stated in these terms.

" It is enough for our purpose to shew that the Company were " *acting in this territory only by virtue of the License.*" It may be quite true that it would be enough for the Respondents' purpose to shew this, but unfortunately for them it is precisely what cannot be shown. They return to it again and again, and although each new attempt meets with the same result, they, nevertheless, cling to it with desperate tenacity ; as it is in fact their only hope for escaping, in part, the weighty responsibility under which they lie towards the Claimants. The whole proposition and argument hinge upon a barefaced assertion, so destitute of support, and so directly contradicted by an overwhelming mass of facts, that no hesitation can be felt in disposing of it. The assumption, indeed, that the Company held their lands and establishments by virtue of the License of Exclusive Trade, is of comparatively recent date. Nothing of the kind is in any manner expressed or intimated in the License itself. It was not so said or implied in the British Statement annexed to the Protocol of 1826, nor in any of the State Documents or correspondence anterior to the Treaty. It is not assumed to be so by the American historian, Greenhow, or any of the writers on the Oregon boundary question. Nothing was said of it in the Treaty, nothing of the kind was ever set up by the British Government, nor indeed by the American, until in 1853 the happy thought occurred to Governor Stevens. It was embodied in his Report, and then seized with avidity by all who were interested in evading the obligations of the Treaty of 1846, and has ever since been produced and reproduced as the great stalking horse of the American argument against the Hudson's Bay Company's claims. Any assumption more utterly unsupported by the facts of the case, or the agreement of delimitation, it would be impossible to conceive. The pretension is that the guarantee given by the third article of the Treaty is, that the Hudson's Bay Company shall be protected in the License of exclusive trade and its incidents, and in nothing more. If nothing was contemplated by the Treaty but the license to trade, why was it not so put ? Why, for a single limited object, make use of such broad terms as " possessory rights " without any reference to this License or to any other limitation ? Is such an interpretation consistent with legal rules or common sense ? But the considerations which contradict this interpretation are so strong and may be put so briefly, that I shall simply enumerate them and leave this utterly absurd pretension without further answer. They are taken chiefly from the opening argument in the case, and will be found in a more extended form on pp. 16, 17, 18 and 21 of that argument, to which the Commissioners are respectfully referred.

1. The Company, at the time of and before the date of the License, was in possession of several important settlements in Oregon: among them were the Posts at Kootanais, Flatheads, Fort George, Okanagan, Spokan and Walla-Walla, all established or acquired long before that time by the North West Company, and all included in the transfer to the Hudson's Bay Company, by the deed of Indenture. Claimants' Doc. Ev. A, 3 pp. 296, 305.

2. The Act of Parliament, 2 Geo. IV. Ch : 66, (1821) declares in its preamble that the competition in the fur trade between the Hudson's Bay Company and the North West Company had been found *for some years past* to be productive of loss to the Companies, of injury to the Indians, and of violence and loss of life, and that more effectual means were necessary for remedying these evils and bringing offenders to justice : upon these considerations the act was passed to authorize the granting of the License and for other purposes.

3. In the License it is declared that the Hudson's Bay Company and North West Company *had respectively extended the fur trade over many parts of North America* which had not been before explored, and repeats the declaration in the Act of Parliament that the competition had been found *for some years past* to be productive of injury. The Deed of Indenture is recognized in the License and made one of the inducements for granting it. The License then was given, not to create a possession and give a consequent title to land, but because the Company already had such possession and title. (See License Doc. Ev. A 5, p. 315).

4. The extent and permanent character of its operations and establishments then existing in Oregon, are indicated by the provision in the License entrusting in a degree to the Company the administration of civil and criminal justice.

5. The British Statement annexed to the Protocol of the 18th December, 1826, alleges that " numerous settlements and trading posts " by British subjects (necessarily meaning the Hudson's Bay and North West Companies) upon the Columbia, and northward and southward of it, *had existed many years*. (Greenhow, p. 451, App. H.)

6. The British Government, long after the revocation of the License, formally confirmed to the Hudson's Bay Company a mos valuable tract of land in the Island of Vancouver, a portion of which was sold in lots by the Company in 1861, at a rate exceeding $2400 an acre, and other portions for £100 sterling an acre, and also numerous Posts in British Columbia, with the land around them—all those lands having been acquired and held precisely as were those on the Columbia river.

7. In addition to all this, it may be said that there is no expression or implication in the License from which title to land or permission to occupy it can be derived. The whole weight of evidence, both documentary and testimonial, shows that the land and etablishments, as also the trade, were held independent of the License, which was a mere incident, intended, as is clearly expressed upon the face of it, to put an end to the disorders arising from the violent competition in trade of two powerful and rival companies.

The License is not a license to trade, for that would have given nothing which the Company did not before possess. It had its trade and it had its establishments necessary for carrying on the trade ; bnt the License gave it what it had not before, viz : a right of excluding all competition in trade except by citizens of the United States. The terms of the instrument shew that its intention was not to introduce a new trade but to protect one which was already established in the country. Now this fact of a pre-existing trade and pre-existing establishment is a conclusive refutation of of the pretension that this trade and these establishments were created by the License aud depended upon it for their existence.

But admitting for the sake of argument that the fact was not so, and that the License was the beginning of the trade of the Company in Oregon—what then ? The License gave a right of exclusive trade, and it gave nothing else. The lands and whatever else were acquired were not given by the License, even if acquired during its continuance and in view of making it more effectual and valuable. They were acquired by acts of appropriation independent of any authority given by the License, viz : by taking possession of cultivating and occupying them, for various purposes. The License gave no title to do this. Having got the Posts, the Company carried on trade at those Posts and throughout the country, and by virtue of the License it excluded others from that trade, but if no such License had existed they would have continued to carry on and extend their trade and to appropriate land and establish Posts— and after the amalgamation with the North West Company, it is likely this would have been done without rivalry. The exclusive right of trade then was one thing, and the possession of the lands altogether another. The trade, but not the right of exclusion, was to a certain extent dependent upon the establishments for being conveniently and profitably carried on, but the right in these establishments was not at all dependent upon the trade. Both the exclusiveness and the trade itself might cease, and still their real estate would remain in the possession of the Company by the title of possession as a " possessory right." This possessory title was of course defeasible by the higher title, but, until so defeated, it was *primâ facie* good against all others. It was not so defeated, but on the contrary was recognized and confirmed in the Treaty of 1846 by both the parties who claimed to hold the paramount title.

I cannot doubt that these reasons will be found conclusive against the attempt of the counsel for the Respondent to confound together and mystify the relations of two things which are perfectly distinct, and independent of each other. It is inconceivable that a mind so highly trained and acute as his, can be deceived by so flimsy a fallacy as the argument upon this pretension presents ; but it is still more inconceivable that he should hope to impose it upon the judgment of the Commissioners.

Having, as I apprehend, successfully disposed of this subject, it is unnecessary to follow the long technical discussion upon the effect of licenses and the rights of licensors and licensees, which covers the pages numbered from 8 to 14, and is backed by a great many citations from the books. My answer to all these is that whether they be right or wrong they have nothing to do with the case. With respect to the revocation of the License, it will be noticed hereafter under No. V and also in connection with the Report of the Committee of the House of Commons under the No. VIII.

IV. This fourth proposition, p. 14, has its foundation upon the same pretension that the License of exclusive trade was the origin and title of the Company's rights, and it falls therefore within the scope of the remarks already made under the foregoing number. The specification of the Company's rights in the paragraphs a, b, and c, is accepted so far as it goes, but it falls far short of their entire extent.

V. This proposition, pp. 15 to 17, is also based upon the same assumption as the preceding one. The definition of the Company's possessory rights may be accepted in so far as the mere land claim is concerned. A few words of explanation of the revocation of the License of exclusive trade in 1859 will show the utter groundlessness of the pretensions of the Respondents founded upon it. By the terms of the second License granted in 1838, a power was reserved by the Crown to establish colonies within the territories covered by it, and for that purpose to revoke the License or any part of it. (Doc. Ev., p. 319).

This revocation became necessary, and was made in accordance with these terms upon the erection of the two colonies of Vancouver's Island and British Columbia in 1859. The fact that the British Government deemed it necessary specially to reserve in the License a sovereign right of this nature, shows how large and comprehensive it considered the rights of the Hudson's Bay Company to be in the country.

The revocation was made as stated upon the erection of the two colonies of Vancouver's Island and British Columbia, but the Respondents are entirely wrong in their facts when they assert that this revocation affected the *status* of the Company in these two colonies. On the contrary, they continued to enjoy all their rights there, except the right of excluding others from the fur trade. The Posts and establishments were undisturbed in both colonies, and they received for them a formal conveyance in fee simple from the British Government. It certainly required great moral or rather immoral courage in the face of these facts to set up the statements and conclusions preferred in behalf of the Respondents under this number V.

VI. This proposition relates to the nature and extent of the obligation of the United States to "respect" the Company's rights. The proposition does not, in the form in which that obligation is put materially differ in principle from the proposition of the Company stated on p. 9, and treated on p. 187 and following pages of the opening argument. " All that the United States were required to do," says the counsel for the Respondents, " was to refrain from " violation *by itself or its officers* of the possessory rights of the " Company, and to permit the Company to enjoy the judicial reme- " dies for individual trespasses customary in the country." The Claimants' statement is that the United States, " *by its officers and* " *citizens, acting uuder the authority of its Government and law,* " have violated and usurped these rights."

There is, it appears, no controversy between us on the point that the United States are liable for the acts of its officers and for acts done under its laws in violation of the rights of thé Company. The only substantial question is whether that Government is liable for the acts of its citizens. I have but a word to say on this question. These acts are of two kinds—either they are acts done by the citizens under authority of the Donation and Settlement or other Laws of the United States, or they are acts of individual trespass not committed under the sanction or color of law. It is for the latter class of acts alone, it appears to me, that any doubt can arise as to the liability of the United States. As a general rule the Government would not be liable. But it is contended and proved that the course pursued by the officers, civil and military, of . . United States, acting in many instances under instructions from the Government, and on all occasions, whether so acting or not, denying everywhere and in the most emphatic manner the rights of the Company, and the whole policy and conduct of the Government towards the Company up to the time of its final expulsion, were such that the population of the country were countenanced and encouraged in all forms of trespass and violation of these rights ; and the United States having thus been the promoter and encourager of them all, is liable to the Company for the consequent injury suffered by it. There is also another consideration connected with the subject of these aggressions, which is not less conclusive. The citizens of the United States who trespassed and *squatted* upon the lands of the Company have either obtained grants of the Sections occupied by them or they have not. If they hold grants, as is the case with nearly all of them, the responsibility of the United States cannot be questioned, for by these grants it has maintained the trespassers and received from them the price of the land. On the other hand, where no grant has yet been made, the land will pass to the United States by the effect of the award to be rendered by this Commission—and the squatter will be liable to pay his government for it. In either case therefore and under any point of view, it is certain that the United States must answer to the Company for these aggressions. For the facts connected with the subject of aggressions, reference is made to p. 207 and following (No. 3), and generally to the pages from 187 to 218 of the opening argument. See also inf. (VII.)

VII. (p. 19) Under this number the counsel for the Respondent asks, "what evidence would prove that the United States invaded "the possessory rights of the Company," and answers; first, when the United States took possession of some portion of land claimed by the Company; or, secondly, permitted donation or pre-emption claims to be located on land claimed by the Company. The pretensions set up under this introduction are little more than a repetition and enlargement of those contained under the former number, and are covered by the remarks made in that connection. The reasoning is as fallacious and manifestly untenable in the one as in the other. There can surely be no doubt of the following as matters of fact: 1st—that the United States Government did appropriate to its own use large tracts of the land possessed by the Company; and 2nd—that a great portion of the land of the Company was located under the donation laws of the United States by its officers. For most, if not all of those locations, patents have been issued. This is apparent from the whole tenor of the evidence in relation to the lands at the more important Posts. The extent to which it was done, even many years ago, at Vancouver, is seen by the official map of Clarke County marked "H," upon which the patented sections are marked "P" in red ink. The records of the Land Office at Washington would have shown the extent of the grants, but access was denied to this source of information, and as the fact sought to be established is but one of a great mass of facts which prove the aggressions complained of, it was not deemed advisable to suffer additional vexatious delay for an object not of essential importance to the case. (See correspondence between counsel, Claimants, Doc. Ev. F 21, F 21a, F 21b, p. 427, et seq).

As to the question whether the United States are liable on the above facts, if the counsel be serious in raising it, I can scarcely believe an answer is required before this tribunal, or indeed any other composed of educated lawyers, to show that a Government is answerable for the acts of its officers in carrying into effect its own laws. The case of Pierce *vs.* United States, cited upon p. 23, has not the least analogy or bearing in the present claim.

The point incidentally put that the Company can claim nothing except what remained in its actual possession, and has lost all which has been taken, or which it has been compelled to abandon, has been fully disposed of in the opening argument.

VIII. Damages (p. 24 to 26). The discussion under this head is based chiefly upon the ever reiterated assertion that the License of Exclusive Trade was the title of the Company. I refer to what has already been said on that subject in the opening argument, and in this reply. There is besides a good deal of labor bestowed in endeavoring to establish a measure of damages which would leave little to be awarded to the claimants, and as auxiliary to this the new form of stating the "possessory rights" of the Treaty as "rights of possession to land alone," is again brought up. The Claimants of course do not acquiesce in this any more than in the other propositions connected with it, which have all been disposed of in the arguments and are overthrown by the evidence, which is abundant on this division of the claim.

(B).—VALUE OF POSTS.

Upon the evidence of record I do not propose again to enter. It was purposely examined and set out with great fullness in the opening argument in order to avoid any lengthened recurrence to it. I leave it therefore without adding to the exposition and reasoning upon it already submitted. I may be permitted, however, to notice the curious fact that the counsel for the Respondents, in arraying his witnesses and giving his view of the evidence for the United States in relation to Vancouver, carefully excludes Mr. A'Hern, the clerk and auditor of Clarke County. That gentleman, from his thorough knowledge, his official situation, which compelled him to a perfect familiarity with the subject on which he spoke, and his freedom from all interest, and certainly from all bias in favor of the claimants, is entitled to be heard with perfect confidence ; and he says the true value of the land on the town site alone of Vancouver in 1866 was $773,070. I commend the evidence of this witness to the consideration of the Commissioners ; as to the rest of the evidence, I am content with requesting only that it may be, as it undoubtedly will be, carefully analysed and weighed.

CONCLUSION AS TO THE POSTS (p. 57 to 64).

This conclusion seems to me to divide itself into two branches— I can scarcely call them propositions. The first presents a labored comparison of the Indian possession of the country with that of the Hudson's Bay Company. The Counsel for the defence comes to the conclusion that they were alike, because the Indian possession is lost with the extinction of the tribe, and the possession of the Hudson's Bay Company, as he asserts, is lost with the expiration or revocation of the License of Exclusive Trade ; and after having built up this card house to his own satisfaction, he nails the whole with this salient and convincing piece of logic : " That this right " of occupancy must be limited in point of duration by the legal con- " tinuance of the License of Trade is clear, *because, unless so limi-* " *ted, there is no limitation to it and it would be perpetual.*" This is an argument *ex necessitate* with a vengeance—Because the pos- session would be perpetual unless it be limited by the Licence, therefore the License *must*, says he, *be made to limit it*, whether by its terms or by the facts which interpret them it does so or not. It has been shown, not once but repeatedly that the legal conti- nuance of the License of Trade had no connection with the pos- sessory rights of the Company guaranteed by the Treaty either in originating or continuing them, but that these rights existed entirely independently of the License, and were by that Treaty made perpetual. What particular application or virtue the Indian possession has had in evolving the great truth announced in this pregnant sentence, I do not fully comprehend, but it is enough that it has given an opportunity for again introducing the unfounded assumption of the Respondents with respect to the License of Trade.

2. The second branch of the " Conclusion " contains an exposition

of the land laws of the United States, as they regulate the rights of the citizens of that Government in their pre-emption of land. It entirely ignores the higher law of Treaty rights, and the obligations assumed under that of 1846 in favor of the claimants. I have nothing to say about the rules of law stated upon this subject, or very many of the other subjects on which, a great deal of learning is displayed ; except that it is misapplied, as these rules do not bear upon the substantial questions raised and discussed in the opening argument, and which alone the Commissioners have to decide. On the contrary, as it seems to me, there is a constant effort to evade those questions by presenting a great variety of bootless discussions upon points which can have, for the most part, no influence upon the decision in this case.

(RIGHT OF TRADE, p. 64).

I. It is worthy of remark, that while the counsel of the Respondents, following Governor Stevens, insists that the License of Exclusive Trade with the Indians is the sole title of the Claimants, and that it limits as it originated their rights, he, at the same time, concurs with the report of that gentleman in denying to the Company the right, not only of exclusive trade, but of any trade at all. I cannot understand how both of these propositions can be true, but will not prolong the discussion by pointing out how contradictory and absurd they both are. The propositions of the Claimants on the subject are :

1. That the right of trade may be a *possessory right*.

2. That such a right was possessed by the Company in 1846 and before, and was included by the Treaty under the expression " possessory rights."

3. That the evidence is abundant to show the nature and extent of that trade, as well with the Indians as others.

I do not intend to enlarge upon these propositions, but refer with confidence to what is said on this subject in the opening argument under the head " Rights of trade." As to the re-iteration by the Respondents of their argument founded upon the pretension that there can be no such thing as a possessory right of trade, because it is not attached to anything which has physical existence, it has already been disposed of, and I do not deem it necessary again to show its futility. But it is said for the Respondents that the right to trade with the Indians was respected by them (p. 68 to 70). This is a mere question of fact, and the Commissioners are referred to that part of the opening argument (pp. 201-2-3-4) where the evidence on that subject is noticed, and where a reference to it will be found. (See also Claimants' Doc. Ev., A 10-A 11, p. 325, C. 2 p. 368).

(D.)—NAVIGATION OF THE COLUMBIA, (p. 70).

I find nothing in what is said for the Respondents under this head or the next, " The Portages" (p. 75), which seems to me to render necessary any addition to what is contained in the opening argument under the same heads, except that it is a very great error on the part of the Respondents' counsel to suppose that it is given up.

(E.)—MISCELLANEOUS POINTS.

I. Remarks on certain witnesses.

As to the character of the witnesses for the Claimants, their relation toward the Company, and their claims upon the confidence of the Commissioners, on the score of social position, of probity, of familiar knowledge, and of connected and sustained statement, enough has been said to enable me to leave the subject with confidence without further enlarging upon it.

To this, however, there is one exception. Mr. Mactavish has been favored with so large a share of attention by the counsel for the Respondents, both in the examination and in the strictures upon his evidence, that I must devote a few words in answer to what has been said of his testimony and of himself.

It was natural that after the astounding *tour de force* of putting 1052 questions for the United States by a three counsel power, some mortification should have been felt that the witness could not be made to contradict himself, or to depart from his sturdy asseveration of the truth. This disappointment was without doubt a distressing one, and hence an attack of corresponding bitterness is made upon the witness. The whole of his evidence and the circumstances of his examination have been treated in the opening argument on the 53rd and following pages. It is made manifest there that he is not alone in his estimates or in any fact which he asserts. He is supported directly or indirectly by all the witnesses for the Claimants who speak upon the same subjects; Lowe, Anderson, McKinlay, Crate and Simmons, sustain him by positive statement which the others corroborate, although in a less direct form. Without doubt there are numerous witnesses for the United States of all conditions and all degrees of credibility from zero upwards, who have made contra statements as well to his evidence as to all the proof produced by the Claimants. Many of these witnesses, as has been shown, are unworthy of belief, and the others had nothing of the familiar knowledge of the subject of which they spoke which was possessed by Mr. Mactavish or the other witnesses for the Claimants. Under these circumstances, the statement that "the testimony of Mr. Mactavish is not "reconcilable with any hypothesis of common truth or good faith, "and stands here in print to his dishonor as a gentleman and a "man," is a gratuitous assertion utterly without warrant or justification. The probity of Mr. Mactavish and his honor as a gentleman, will bear favorable comparison with that of any man whose name has figured in the array of witnesses or counsel in this long drawn out case, and he has not the least reason to fear that it will suffer from anything to be found in the record.

I shall add no more on this subject, but I will notice in this connection, in order to have done with it, a *tripartite* letter between Mr. Gibbs, Mr. Cushing and Mr. Beaman, respecting the first named gentleman. I do not well understand how these letters are to be considered as making part of the record, but the combined production is a singular one, and adds a good deal of force to what has been said of Mr. Gibbs' position and evidence in the opening argument. To the letters in so far as they are intended to censure the Counsel for the Claimants I shall of course say nothing. It would be a violation of self-respect and respect for the Commissioners to do so. Concerning my strictures on Mr. Gibbs' evidence, I reviewed it from itself alone, stating nothing which is not borne out by the record. As to insinuations, I made none—I meant none. I thought Mr. Gibbs' intemperate zeal for one party, and hostility to the other, had led him to place himself in an extraordinary and unjustifiable position and I think so still. Outside of the record, I have no reason and certainly have no wish to speak otherwise than kindly of Mr. Gibbs. His ability and varied knowledge I willingly admit, and acknowledge his uniform courtesy in all my intercourse with him.

III. Suppression of Accounts by the Company, (p. 90).

The allegation of suppression of evidence involved in this title is met at once by an emphatic and unqualified denial. The assertion is utterly without foundation. There has been no suppression of accounts, or of any other evidence by the Claimants, which is more than can be truly said on the part of the defence.

The first point offered under this head, by the defence, is that the books of account showing the cost of the improvements have not been produced (p. 91). The simple and conclusive reason why they were not produced is, that there are no books of account showing the amounts expended for the buildings and improvements at the different Posts. These improvements were not made and completed ever as one exclusive work, but went on from year to year—the great body of men in the service of the Company working at them, not exclusively or constantly, but from time to time as was found convenient. This is distinctly stated by Mr. Mactavish in his evidence, pp. 46, 48, 49, and in various other portions of it. He coincides in these statements with Sir James Douglas, p. 52, and he is sustained by the evidence of Roberts, pp. 14, 15, 16, Ev. for U. S. Miscellaneous, and by Armit. Indeed, it is admitted by the Respondents, through one of their Counsel, that " it is " evident from an examination of the books that no account was kept " of the cost of erecting and repairing Posts. The only accounts " returned from the districts and Posts being servants' wages, and " the goods expended for labor and trade, which were set off against " the furs returned, and the profit of the year thus arrived at." This was after a thorough inspection of the books by the " attorney and agent of the United States," with Dr. Tolmie, and certainly must be deemed a conclusive answer to this bold charge of suppressing accounts. (See pp. 189, 190, Ev. for the U. S. Miscellaneous).

A word must be here said, however, with reference to the application made to Dr. Tolmie to extend the memorandum which regulated the subjects on which the archives and books of the Company at Vancouver were to be inspected, and his letter in answer quoted

(p. 92). The memorandum A, p. 191 Miscellaneous Ev. U. S., is a simple copy made by the counsel for the Claimants from one furnished by the senior counsel for the United States, who might have embraced in it whatever he pleased, so that the examination could have been confined within any reasonable limit of time ; and no objection would have been made. It is obvious that in an investigation covering so large a ground and so many years as this has, some declaration was necessarily required from the Respondents' counsel as to the subjects and dates on which he was to examine the hundreds of volumes of books of account. Without a check of that description the task would never have been terminated. The memorandum mentioned above was sent to Victoria, and a considerable length of time was consumed in the examination under it. Then a new requisition was made, not to the Company's counsel but to Dr. Tolmie, and he, seeing the delay that would necessarily accrue from this new proceeding, declined to go further than his instructions warranted. After this the agreement (p. 189) dated April 18th was signed by him and the local counsel for the United States. No further application was made and nothing more was heard upon the subject. It is evident from a glance at the items 1, 2, 3, of the supplementary requisition, that the Company had nothing to fear from the inspection of their books or documents on those subjects, nor had they indeed on any other; but as there seemed to be a fixed intention to prolong this case as far as possible and to embarrass it with extraneous and irrelevant matter, it was deemed necessary that some specific definition of what was required should be obtained and acted upon, and this more especially because the Respondents had put in no written answer to the memorial of the Claimants. All the information which could have been furnished upon that requisition and have been utilized by the Respondents, is in fact upon the record.

A third imputation made under this head is, like its predecessors, without foundation; it relates to the taking of evidence in London (p. 93). The counsel for the Claimants believed that valuable information might be derived from the older officers at that place. But it was found after some correspondence that nothing could be proved there of material importance to either party. The counsel for the Respondents, however, insisted upon going there, and the business was entrusted to a gentleman of high connections, who I dare say enjoyed a pleasant trip. No obstruction was put in the way of access to the books or to any other sources of information; on the contrary, every facility was offered. I refer for confirmation of this fact to the letters of Mr. Seward (Miscellaneous Ev. of U. S., pp. 9, 10). The result was that some useful evidence was obtained for the Claimants. I cannot omit here to thank the learned counsel for relieving the dreariness of this discussion by his page of elaborate drollery about mother country, old gentlemen with quills behind their ears, and all the rest of it. The Commissioners cannot fail to appreciate the little story, for it is not only droll, but has the virtue (rare in comic stories) of being about as veracious and as good a substitute for just reasoning, as most of the graver portions of the argument.

The manner in which the counsel for the United States takes leave of Mr. Mactavish (pp. 95, 96), is so plaintive that I must invite for it special attention. After being foiled, as he himself states, in all his super-lawyer-like struggles to compel this devoted witness to prove a fact which did not exist, and to involve him in self-contradiction, he retires from the field of his discomfiture under cover of the portentous question (962), in which he requires the witness to produce *there* " *all accounts, account* " *books, and letter books which were kept at the various Posts of* " *the Company south of the 49th parallel of north latitude during* " *their occupation.*" Now this occupation, be it known, covered some forty years in time. The number of the Posts was at least fourteen. It is not too much to say therefore that the books must have amounted to some thousands of volumes. It is no wonder that the witness, bewildered by such a wild and monstrous demand as this, should have declared his utter inability to say what he would do. If he had said no, there would have been a half or perhaps a whole dozen of pages denouncing the Company in the most indignant terms for suppressing evidence; if—and I tremble while I write it —he had said yes, the mere getting of these books from their places into the chambers of this Commission, if that had been possible, would have occupied I know not what measure of time and money; and when this great feat had been achieved, the invaluable life of the learned counsel might have been ingloriously consumed in poring through these fatal volumes to find what they never contained—a worse fate surely than that pursuit of knowledge under difficulties with Mr. Mactavish which he so affectingly deplores. In sober truth, the demand made in this interrogatory (952) was, under the circumstances, one of the most unreasonable and extravagant that could well be conceived, and it met with precisely the answer which it merited.

V.—MOTION IN AMENDMENT (p. 104).

Nothing is advanced under this head which constitutes any legal objection to the motion fyled by the Claimants, although there is a good deal of injurious and somewhat declamatory imputation against the Company. It is a kind of proceeding perfectly well recognized and of daily occurrence in the Courts. It was made at the proper time, that is, when all the evidence was before the Court, and the result of the proof was manifestly such as to justify an increase of the demand. The menace of re-opening the case is idle—no such right results from a motion of this nature. It is curious that the counsel for the Respondents should be so much alarmed by the motion, when, less indulgent even than Governor Stevens, he considers $250,000 to be a large estimation of the rights of this Company and the Puget Sound Agricultural Company together.

VI. THE COMPANY's OWN ESTIMATE OF ITS VALUE, p. 106 et seq.

Upon the subject of offers and negotiations ending with the letter of Lord Lyons of Dec. 10th 1860, (Mis. Ev., U. S. p. 284.) I shall add nothing to what has been said in the opening argument on pages numbered from 221 to 230, where I have given the history of these negotiations and the circumstances under which they were made. The account there given is a perfectly true one, and I believe it to be conclusive in shewing that they ought not in reason or law to have any influence upon the decision in this case.

But the Counsel for the Respondents fancies he has discovered other estimates on which he can build an argument, and he raises any number of fanciful and abstruse arithmetical problems in the effort to do so. It will be easy to shew the great and palpable error of all these elaborate calculations, and to demonstrate that the learned Counsel has fallen into a lamentable state of self mystification. Turn and twist the figures as he may and enliven the process with all forms of invective and objurgation against the Claimants, the position still remains the same. The arithmetic does them no more harm than does the invective; his figures of speech and figures of numeration are equally innocuous.

The first set of figures upon which the Respondents fasten as containing an estimate by the Claimants of the value of their possessory rights which bars them from recovering any larger amount, is the statement produced before the Committee of the House of Commons, and printed in the Appendix to their Rep. p. 449. I do not take it as quoted on p. 108 of the Respondents' argument, because it is imperfectly given there. The item alluded to is in the following terms: "*Property and investments* in the territory of Oregon *ceded to the United States* by the Treaty of 1846," and which were secured to the Company as possessory rights under that Treaty. I have but a few words to say on the subject of this item. In the first instance, I would call attention to its peculiar wording, " property and investments ceded to the United States," which is a misstatement; and again to the uncertain manner in which the amount is stated, " $1,000,000, say £200,000 stg.," showing an inaccuracy in carrying out and converting one denomination of currency into another of not less than $26,000, and indicating how little importance was attached to the figures named. Both these loose forms of statement show that the document by whomsoever prepared, is not to be relied upon as really an exponent of the rights of the Company.

The fact is, that although it was necessary to include some mention of the claim in the statement, in order to show that it was still unsatisfied, yet the investigation had no reference to that claim, and no mortal sagacity was competent to make even a remote guess of its real value at that time. Between Sir George Simpson's estimate of $1,233,000, exclusive of the navigation of the Columbia, and that of Governor Stevens of $300,000, backed by Mr. Secretary Marcy, a great variety of sums had been discussed from the year 1852, to the date of the statement, 8th June, 1857. As to the $300,000, the Congress of the United States had in 1855, refused to make provision for paying that sum or any other. Mr. Crampton and Mr. Lumley, representing the British Government at Washington, had expressed at different times their opinion that it was the intention of the United States Government to take the property without paying for it, and the officers of the Company felt the same apprehension. (See opening argument pp. 224-225, and references there made). What the claim was then really worth it was impossible to estimate. From the doubtfulness of ever being paid, it seemed worth little or nothing, and was, in fact, probably so considered. But the figures given, though given blindly and evidently without any intelligent comprehension of the matter, afford no countenance or shadow of support to the Respondents' pretensions. The words of the statement do not comprise the right of trade, nor the right of navigating the Columbia, and it must be carefully noted that in this item no allusion is made to the rights of the Puget Sound Agricultural Company. It is nakedly the property and investments, and these are put at a venture, at $1,000,000.

Now, if the claims of the Hudson's Bay Company alone were valued at that amount, independently of the rights of trade and the rights of navigation, when no provision had been made or was likely to be made, for securing the payment of them, and there was little or no hope of their being recovered, it is not too much to say that the amount demanded and proved as their value in the present case is less than truth and justice would warrant, now that under the Treaty of 1863, and before this commission, a certain and effectual mode of recovery is provided. That which before was a feeble hope of obtaining little, if anything, has now become a fixed certainty of obtaining what is justly due ; the whole difference between a bad or very doubtful debt and a good one.

I now pass to the second array of figures in which the Respondents profess to find evidence of bad faith and false valuation on the part of the Claimants (p. 109 to p. 121). These figures will be found in connection with the formation of the "International Financial Company," stated in the Prospectus of that Company. (Mis. Ev. U. S., p. 21). In this latter effort they are even more unfortunate, if possible, than in the former essay, for here the counsel has really nothing but his own erroneous assumptions to rest upon. In the whole thing he has fallen into a gross and manifest mistake, which it is only necessary to point out in order to shew how groundless his pretensions are.

The simple fact is, that the claim against the United States was not included at all in the statement in the Prospectus relied upon by the Respondents. That it was not, is clear from the most cursory examination of the prospectus itself. It is not pretended, of course, that it was included in the second item : " The landed territory of the Company, held under their Charter," &c., but it is most unwarrantably asserted that this claim makes part of the assets of the Company stated in the first item to amount to £1,023,569. There is not a shadow of proof that the claim was included in this item, and a comparison of the statement in the Prospectus with that given to the Committee of the House of Commons, shews a difference of a little more than the $1,000,000, at which the claim was put in the latter, indicating the exclusion of that claim, which was in the former estimate, from the one given in the prospectus.

But this is not all, the Prospectus itself negatives the assumption. In going on to particularize the extent and peculiar advantages of the assets and property to be invested in the new adventure, an enumeration is given of them, beginning on p. 21. The assets of the Company, it is there said, " *will consist of goods in the interior, on shipboard, and other stock in trade, including shipping, business premises, and other buildings necessary for carrying on the fur trade ;*" and, "in addition to its chartered territory, the Company " possesses the following landed property : several plots of land in " British Columbia, occupying most favorable sites at the mouths of " rivers, the titles to which have been confirmed by Her Majesty's " Government, farms, building sites in Vancouver's Island and in " Canada, ten square miles at Lacloche on Lake Huron, and tracts " of land at fourteen other places." But these plots of land do not any more than the claim upon the United States make part of the assets stated in the Prospectus.

How is it possible in the face of these plain enumerations, among which not the slightest allusion is found to any claim against the United States, to have fallen into so palpable an error, as the assumption that the present claim was included within it. But if these indications had been less clear, it seems to me, that a moment's consideration would convince any reasonable mind that the claim could not have been included in that Prospectus. An assignment of it to the new Company would have been, at least, a perilous experiment in the face of all the difficulties, evasions and opposition which the claim even in the hands of its original holders was sure to meet, and it would most: probably have become utterly valueless to the assignees. Then what kind of an asset could this litigious claim have been considered ; for the Prospectus was issued before intelligence of the Treaty of 1863 could have reached England (Armit's Ev. p. 18, Mis. Ev. U. S.), when all was in doubt about it, and when, indeed, the condition of public affairs in the United States and the relations of the two countries toward each other, justified the worst forebodings. The putting down under these circumstances of the claim under the Treaty as an asset and part of the capital stock in the endeavor to float a new adventure, would have been a novel experiment which no man of common sense would have been likely to venture upon. There can be no shadow of doubt, that by prudent design the claim was not in any degree or manner, directly or indirectly, included or referred to in that statement or prospectus. The matter is too plain to require further argument, or perhaps to have required any, and thus all the ingenious hypotheses, elaborate arithmetic and fine spun inferences of the Respondents, fall hopelessly to the ground.

VII. REMARKS ON LEGAL OPINIONS IN FAVOR OF THE COMPANY,
(p. 121).

It would be an unprofitable consumption of time to follow the counsel for the Respondents in his review of the opinions cited by the Claimants in their opening argument. They are the opinions of men eminent as lawyers, and some of them distinguished as statesmen and legislators. The imputation cast upon them, and upon the whole legal profession by the remarks contained on the 122nd page of the argument, exhibits a lax code of professional morality which the higher class of lawyers in all countries will be unwilling to acknowledge. The meaning of the imputation is, that lawyers, of whatever rank or standing, will sell opinions which they know to be unfounded and false, to any body who can pay for them. Having laid down this extraordinary principle of professional ethics to his own satisfaction, the counsel then proceeds to the examination of the several opinions given, but he fails to show that they are either false or unfounded. It would be a wearisome and useless infliction upon the Commissioners to go over all this ground again, and, therefore, these opinions are left, as may safely be done, to speak for themselves upon the objections which are proposed against them. It may, however, be observed that the basis of much of the argument for the Respondents in controverting these opinions consists: 1st of the ever repeated and ever refuted assumption that the Company held its possessions in Oregon under the License of Exclusive Trade ; and, 2nd, upon the assumption which has been shown to be equally untenable, that the Territory south of the 49th parallel of north latitude, belonged to the United States before the Treaty of 1846, " was always American territory." Without the basis of these two unfounded assumptions, the argument amounts to nothing, and as the radical misconception and error on these points have been more than once fully demonstrated the whole argument is without force. The recurrence on pp. 126-128, to the revocation of the License in 1858, needs no further notice. It has been already shown to have been done in conformity with the terms of the instrument itself, for the purpose of establishing the Colonial Governments of Vancouver's Island and British Columbia, and that the possessory rights of the Claimants were there respected by the British Government. Without dwelling further upon the matters presented under this head, I pass to the next.

VIII. Authoritative.opinions adverse to the Company, (p. 134).

The Counsel for the Respondents, after some introductory remarks under this head and the quotation of a portion of the evidence of Mr. Ellice before the Committee of the House of Commons, asks why the counsel for the Claimants did not cite the opinions of the great lawyers mentioned by Mr. Ellice, instead of the opinions of Mr. Bibb ? The answer is easy and conclusive. The simple reason is, that the opinion of Mr. Bibb is applicable to the present claim, and the opinions of the others named are not. Of all upon the list of illustrious names given by Mr. Ellice, and repeated by the Respondents' counsel, (p. 136), not one, so far as is known to the counsel of the Claimants, has given an opinion which touches any point material to the issue in the present claim. All these opinions had reference to a different controversy and a different class of questions. If not, and there be anything applicable to the present claim, and favorable to the Respondents, why have they not produced it? Certainly, the opinion of the law officers in England, given in 1857, which they have selected for publication, (p. 137), and which, therefore, must be deemed the best they could find for their purpose shows nothing which affects it.

After this question we have again the License of Exclusive Trade, (p. 157). The sweeping assertion with respect to the tenor of the Report of the Committee of the House of Commons (p. 153) is denied. The Report does no such thing as is alleged of it. It was, without doubt, hostile enough in spirit to the Hudson's Bay Company, but it does not appear from it, as is rashly affirmed, that in the Indian Territory the Company held nothing but license to trade, and that whatever the Company did, " whatever it " acquired, and whatever it held, it did, acquired and held solely and " exclusively in virtue of its terminable license to trade, as granted " by the British Crown." All this is untrue. The report, I repeat, decides no such questions. The direct object of the Parliamentary inquiry was to ascertain whether it was advisable to erect Colonial Governments in any portion of the Territory lying within the limits defined by the Charter of the Hudson's Bay Company, or beyond those limits, but covered by the License of exclusive trade; and whether in view of this object, it was, or was not, expedient to extend the term of the License. The decision announced in the Report is, that a portion of the Territory ought to be colonized, (see clause No. 10. of the Report, p. 4; also printed in Sup. and App. of Respondents, p. 15.) and after arriving at that conclusion, we find in Nos. 11 and 12 of the Report, the recommendation of the committee with respect to the Territory covered by the license. This recommendation is to the effect, that for the purpose of maintaining *law and order*—and of preventing the fatal effects of *competition in the fur trade*—and the indiscriminate destruction of the more valuable fur-bearing animals.—" It is desirable that they (The Hudson's Bay Company), should continue to enjoy the privileges of exclusive trade which they now possess: except so far as those privileges are limited by the foregoing recommendations."

As to the words in the Report (p. III) " Land held by License or the Indian Territory," they must, of course, be taken with reference to the subject then under consideration. That subject was not title to lands, but the exclusive right of trade. There were two titles under which the Company claimed that right over different territories: the one was its Charter, covering all the original Hudson's Bay Territory, the other was the License covering what was called the Indian Territory. The terms of the Report were used briefly to distinguish between these two titles of exclusive trade, and the different territories which they respectively covered; they had no reerence to any question of title to land, which was not in any way before the Committee; their object being, as before stated, to inquire to what extent it was expedient to terminate the exclusive right of trade under the License with a view to colonization. Taking together the whole of the article 5 of the report, in which these words occur, it will be manifest that no question of title to farms or other specific portions of land was contemplated by the language then used. It was not necessary perhaps to say so much upon this form of expression, for even if the Committee had declared an opinion as to the nature of the Claimants' title to their lands and other possessions, it would have been a mere opinion and no authority for the Commissioners in the decision of this case. The Government of the day went beyond the Report of the Committee, and availed itself of the right of revoking the License according to the Reservation contained in it, but it never occurred to that Government to confiscate the property real or personal of the Company; how far from it, has appeared in the grants made in Vancouver's Island and British Columbia. The fact is that the revocation of the License was regarded as of little importance; of how little it was considered by those interested in and familiar with the whole business, has already been shewn, and will futher appear by Mr. Ellice's answers to the Ints. 6007 and 6008 of his examination, p. 347, and by passages in Sir John Pelly's letter, quoted in Supp. and App. to Respondent's Argument, p. 24 and 26. In the latter he says: "No substantial benefit is "likely to arise from the License beyond the probable means of "affording peace to our own territories."

As to the Despatches of Sir Edward Bulwer Lytton, including that quoted on p. 138, they have been noticed and accounted for in the opening Argument, p. 229.

IX. PARLIAMENTARY INVESTIGATION OF THE COMPANY.

This heading seems to be introduced for the purpose of admitting some four or five pages of inaccurate historical narrative and declamatory invective. I leave the Counsel for the Respondents to the full credit and enjoyment of it.

X. Photographs, Maps and Plates.

Of the Photographs produced by the Respondents, I have little to say. It cannot escape the attention of the Commissioners that representations of this kind depend entirely upon the aspects in which they are taken. As giving an idea of the structure and value of buildings they are worthless, and I must confess it appears to me to indicate great desperation in the defence to have resorted to such a mode of sustaining it and I cannot but regard the production of them as a puerile experiment. With these bad pictures for evidence and Horace for their law, the Respondents arrive at the conclusion of their argument.

(F.)—CONCLUSION (p. 150.)

This heading covers only an enumeration of the pretensions discussed at length in the preceding pages. It is unnecessary to go over them in detail; all of them which run counter to the claim have been more than once refuted in the course of this discussion, and shown to be without foundation, either as affirmations of fact or propositions of law.

Under No. 24 however there is a repetition in a slightly modified form of the argument founded upon the statement of the International Financial Company. The error with respect to that statement, and the consequent worthlessness of the argument have been fully exposed; but as the writhing and contortions of the defence are manifold and constantly reproduced with slight variations of mis-statement, it may be well to notice this new form of the old fallacy. The whole of this second elaborate piece of arithmetic, settling the entire question at issue by the rule of three, is based upon the same mistake, that the claim of the Company against the United States was included in the sum given as the amount of assets of the International Financial Company in 1863. Having once exposed that error, I need add nothing here; but there are some words in italics on page 155 which invite attention, and I notice them in order to put the facts on their true footing. These words are, "the list includes Nisqually and Cowlitz, set down as establishments of the Hudson's Bay Company." This is perfectly true, but of no importance. The sole object of the paper referred to, was to show the total number of the Indian population. This is evident, from the title "Indian Population," and the preamble or introduction following the title. [see App. to Report of Com. H. C. page 365-6]. It is also evident from the Int. 1471 under which the statement was produced. The posts were mentioned in order only to show the number of Indians who frequented them and nothing more. In order to comprise all these places frequented by Indians and thus give the whole population, the two posts of Nisqually and Cowlitz, which had originally belonged to the Hudson's Bay Company were included in the same list, but this surely does not make them the property of the Hudson's Bay Company, or in any way deprive the Puget Sound Company of their property or possessory rights in them. It is a matter which would not have deserved mention, were it not that the emphatic italics in which the words are exhibited shew that great reliance is placed upon them by the Counsel for the Respondents.

I have now done with the body of the Respondents' argument but have a little to say upon the "Supplement and Appendix," which accompany it. The first portion of it which I shall notice is that under the numbers following.

III and IV. Relation of Trade License to Land Claims.

This is a recurrence to the old pretension, which it is now sought to sustain by certain answers given by the late Sir George Simpson and Mr. Ellice in their evidence before the Committee of the House of Commons. Several pages (7-8-9) are occupied in exhausting a remarkably rich vocabulary of abuse upon these gentlemen and upon those among the Claimants' witnesses whose evidence is most damaging to the Respondents. There is no occasion to offer any defence for either the living or the dead. The memory of the latter is not likely to suffer from so unjustifiable an onset, and as to the former the record is here to shew that, with respect to them, the attack is as groundless as it is virulent. It would be a waste of time to dwell upon this piece of intemperate invective. The evidence upon which it purports to rest will be found, that of Sir George Simpson on pages numbered from 44 to 109 and that of Mr. Ellice from 322 to 333 of the Report of the Committee of the House of Commons.

The portion of the Examination of Sir Geo. Simpson, extracted from the Report and printed on the pages 10, 11, 12 of the Supplement and Appendix of the Respondents, exhibits without doubt, a very confused state of ideas in his mind upon the nature and effect of the License. He evidently confounds the right of exclusive trade, which it gives, with other rights which it did not give, and which were acquired independently of it. The questions and answers under the searching and unfriendly but logical examination, show that his view of the matter was wholly wrong, and not only wrong in fact, but that what he stated could not in the nature of things be correct. As truly put by Mr. Roebuck, the License of exclusive trade gave, and could give no title to land, and if it gave a title to any, it would give it to the whole territory. But what influence is this confused statement of Sir George Simpson expected to have in the case? At the most it was but an opinion, and one evidently seen, upon the mere stating of it, to be wrong. It is also shown to be wrong, by the mass of testimony adduced by the Claimants, and the absolute, inevitable conclusion resulting from the public documents and acts enumerated on p. 16 of the opening argument, and equally so by the inclusion of " all British subjects" in the 2rd. article, and the expression, farms, &c., " belonging to," used in the 4th article of the Treaty in relation to the Puget Sound Agricultural Company, neither of these parties having any license to trade. If every witness before the Committee had sworn that the License of trade was the title of the Company to the lands held in possession by them, it could not have destroyed the facts : 1st, That the License gave no title to lands, and, 2nd, that a portion of their lands was held by the Company before the existence of the first License ; while those acquired afterwards coincidently with the existence of the License, and as auxiliary to its more effectual use, were acquired by a possession which could equally well have existed without it, and was held independently of it. I cannot believe that it is necessary to say more on this incessantly repeated topic.

The despatches of Sir E. B. Lytton, which are again brought up on p. 12 B. have already been disposed of, as have also the Report of the Committee of the House of Common, printed under the numeral V, and the opinions of the Attorney and Solicitor General under No. VI.

Of the papers produced under the numerals which follow to VIII, some have been already noticed, and the others require no notice. As to the recent article from the Westminster Review, printed under No. XIII, p. 42, it fails to strike me as likely to have any influence upon the decision in this case. Why it was republished, it is not easy to say, unless it was with the benevolent intention of putting before the Commission, its true testimony to the wise and philanthropic course pursued by the Hudson's Bay Company in its relations to the Indians. The passage on page 58 commencing with, "Let the proprietors be compensated for the loss of their property," and ending with the words, "most favorable contrast to the reckless dealings of the American Fur Companies," is commended to the notice of the Commissioners.

XIV. MR. APPLEGATE'S LETTER TO GOVERNOR WOODS.

This is the last paper in the Appendix which arrests attention, and that not because it has anything in it to affect the case, but because it is another patriotic production from that zealous but not discreet citizen, Mr. Jesse Applegate. I have already bestowed enough of attention upon this officious gentleman, to make it unnecessary to say much upon this new and striking production.

Mr. Applegate's appearances in this case are multiform. First, we have him figuring in a letter to Governor Gibbs, which will be found in Doc. Ev. of Claimants, p. 483. In that letter he condescendingly tells the Commissioners what he would do if he were one of them. He "would refuse to consider the claim of the Hudson's Bay Company as based upon the Memorial;" and on p. 484, he is of opinion the Company is not entitled to any compensation. Next we have him in the place of his aspiration, really a commissioner, not appointed, it is true, by either Government, but by friendly agreement between himself and the counsel for the United States. He afterwards appears as a witness, in which character he is less successful than in either that of the Governor's correspondent or *pseudo* Commissioner, and with his coadjutors Carson and Rinearson, leaves the stage with anything but credit. Now, however he has revived sufficiently to assist the counsel for the Respondents with this edifying letter to Governor Woods. I have no idea of answering this pretentious and vapid document. The statements, or rather mis-statements in it, can have no weight; for the fact is, that besides the reckless partizanship of the man, he is constitutionally inaccurate and rarely gets his facts right. Instances of this are found in his first letter and in the present one. It is curious to note how many blunders he has crowded into four lines, (p. 62-68.) The Hudson's Bay Company, he says, extended its trade to the West of the Rocky Mountains, by the authority of a license granted by the Prince Regent (afterwards George IV.), he thinks in 1799. Now there was no trade of the Hudson's Bay Company west of the Rocky Mountains for many years after 1799. There was no Regency in that year nor within a period of ten years after. No license was granted in that year, and when granted it was not for twenty years, but for twenty-one. It was not renewed in 1819, nor in 1839, and did not expire in 1859. The native presumption which enables a man to obtrude himself upon a court of competent judges, with his instructions and advice as to their decision, and falls into such a series of continuous blunders, presents in the words of the learned counsel, who has produced him " a curious " subject of psychological investigation." Mr. Applegate, however, grows more merciful the longer he considers the subject, for while in his first letter he would not allow the Commissioners to award anything at all to the Claimants, in the present one he kindly consents to the munificent sum of $50,000.

I cannot but think that the able and distinguished counsel for the United States has betrayed his sense of the weakness of his own argument in thus seeking to sustain it by the production of one from this volunteer advocate, which, however, is weaker still.

I now take leave of this case, but it is due to those whom I represent not to do so without a brief notice of the peculiar style and spirit of the language of the Respondents' argument and of very many of the papers which have been put of Record. It was of course not to be wondered at, that under the strong local prejudice which exists on the western side of the Rocky Mountains and amid the ruder manners which prevail in a new country, such intemperate and coarse attacks should be made as are found in the productions of Gray, Applegate, Hewitt and other caterers for the popular taste in Washington Territory, but it was hardly to be expected that the same defamatory language should have been continued in the defence before a tribunal constituted like the present one. This kind of language, it must be observed, is directed against a Company, the immediate Governing Body of which is composed of men of distinguished social and public position in England, and among whom are some of the foremost of their day in ability, character and rank. Under the authority and instructions of these men the claim has been made and prosecuted up to the present period. Yet it is, says the counsel for the United States, " The sublimity of impudence ;" " Its unimaginable ravenousness passes the limits of indignation " and reaches the region of ridicule and contempt ;" " Grasping, " rapacious, exorbitant and presumptuous ;" " Bogus claim ;" " Audacious and stupendous fraud ;" " Fraudulent excess and attempted extortion ;" these are only some of the energetic and picturesque phrases of abuse, which are spread with a liberal hand over the paper.

I am sorry that this course should have been pursued, not because retort is difficult, for it is easy to say bitter things. The power to insult by injurious epithets and calumnious charges lies within the meanest capacity. But the exercise of such power is grossly out of place in this controversy and before this tribunal. It assuredly will not be received by the Commissioners as a substitute for argument, and can add no strength to the pretensions of the party resorting to it.

I have but a word to say in conclusion upon the character of the defence. It has been got up with great labour and of course with great ability and learning. But it fails to meet the claim. It is discursive and evasive, elaborate on points of little or no application to the questions at issue, subtle and fallacious on those which touch the essentials of the case. It abounds in bold mis-statements and in scandalous invective, and is upon the whole an exceedingly vigorous and true expression of the spirit of aggression and confiscation which has from the beginning of this long protracted quarrel, offered wrong and injury in the place of protection, and insult in answer to just claims for redress. I leave it all, however, with a reassertion of unshaken confidence, that " no " legal subtlety—no ingenuity of argument, no form of sophism can

" so pervert the plain facts of the case, as to free the United States
" Government from full responsibility in this matter."

In concluding I again respectfully solicit the notice of the Commissioners to the great expense which the Claimants have suffered in
consequence of the unjust course pursued by the Respondents in
resisting this claim, and urge that such outlay be taken into consideration by them in making their award. As stated in the
opening argument, the amount has not fallen short of $80,000.
That it must be very large is manifest from the record itself, without
other verification, but more than the sum specified can be sub-
stantiated by vouchers whenever required.

CHAS. D. DAY,
Counsel for the H. B. Co.

Joint Commission on the Claims of the Hudson's Bay and Puget's Sound Agricultural Companies.

To the Honorable the Commissioners:

A few observations will suffice in reply to those offered by the Counsel for the United States, in relation to the negotiations for the transfer of the territory of the Hudson's Bay Company, which terminated in the acceptance by the Company of the terms dictated by the Government of Great Britain, in the letter from the Colonial Office, dated 9th March, 1869.

These negotiations, or their result, cannot be received as affording any kind of evidence or indication of value of the Company's claims against the United States. They involve a variety of considerations and influences, which are entirely independent of any estimate of the value of the soil.

The statements which follow, will be found to be amply borne out, not only by the letter just noticed, but also by reference to a pamphlet recently published in London, entitled "Correspondence between Her Majesty's Government and the Hudson's Bay Company," in which the course and history of all the negotiations from the beginning may be seen. I call attention to the letters from successive Secretaries for the Colonies, and from the Governors of the Hudson's Bay Company, or to particular passages of them contained in it. The references following in the course of these observations are to the pages of this pamphlet.

The considerations and influences alluded to are political and social.

1. It is manifest that so great a territory could not have continued to be held by a private corporation merely for the purpose

of the fur trade. It was necessary that it should be colonized for more general purposes, and that a government emanating from the sovereign authority should take the place of the rule of the Company which was no longer adapted to the wants of settlers there or to the progress of civilization.

2. The Imperial Gov⸱ nt insisted upon this change, and unequivocally intimated that ⸱ Company must yield to the obvious necessities of national policy.

3. The Dominion of Canada persistently urged upon the Imperial Government its demands, that the territory should be made over to the Canadian Government without any settlement of the rights of the Company, to be dealt with according to the discretion of that Government, which manifestly, from all the correspondence on the subject, is very hostile to its claims.

4. There is an universal pressure of public opinion adverse to the Company, making itself felt by an almost unanimous expression in Parliament and through the public press.

5. There is inside the Company a powerful advocacy of the pretensions of the Canadian Government founded not upon commercial, but upon political and other incidental motives.

6. The pressure was not confined to subjects of the British Empire ; an American population is advancing like a wall to the Territory, and if left in its present state would overrun and take possession of it. This must have lead to one of two results, either a total loss of it to the Company or the danger of a war between the two countries.

7. The refusal to accept the terms offered would, upon the most favorable view, have involved the Company in the responsibility of establishing and maintaining at a great expense a Provincial Government in the Territory, similar to those in other portions of the Empire.

Under all these circumstances and influences, which have nothing to do with the question of true value, the best friends of the Company may feel that it would have been unwise to neglect the offer accepted by it, or almost any other offer which might have been made.

It is certain that this great corporation and monopoly has outlived its time, in so far as its exclusive possession of so great a territory for the sole purposes of its trade is concerned, and that it must yield to the force of circumstances. The amount of compensation which has been fixed, depended not upon any estimation that it may have made of its property, however moderate and just, but simply upon the forbearance and sense of justice which those who held the power felt disposed under very great and increasing pressure to observe.

This is apparent from the fact that one Secretary for the Colonies in 1868, would have given £1,000,000 with one tenth of the soil and freedom from taxation. Another in 1869, without any change in the value of the property or any assignable reason, other than those which I have stated, offered only £300,000 and one twentieth of the land, and this in terms too peremptory to be misunderstood. Meanwhile Canada was persistently and strongly urging that nothing at all should be given: and the sudden and enormous reduction of £700,000 from the former offer might have well excited a doubt as to what in this rapidly descending scale any succeeding offer might be.

Now the presence of all these incidental considerations and influences is foreign to the question to be decided in the present claims. The sole question here is not one connected with political expediency or in any manner dependent upon the stringent requirements of national policy, but is merely one of actual value of property dependent upon fertility of the soil, advantages of situation, facility of access, surrounding population and all the other circumstances which make one tract of land worth more than another as land, and these which are the sole legitimate grounds of decision in the present claims, were of little weight or of none whatever in the negotiations for acquiring the Hudson's Bay Territory.

It is moreover to be remembered that the Company could have but one purchaser.

The negotiations with a Company of American speculators was discouraged by the Imperial Government, and although the expressions used have the conventional moderation of official correspondence in England, it is certain that a sale would not have been permitted (p. 82 to 87.) If the Company could have offered the territory to foreign nations as well as to Great Britain and Canada, there would have been a competition from which a very different result as to value would have been obtained, and no nation would have bid higher than the United States. If that Government was willing to give $7,000,000 for a country so remote and isolated and of so little comparative value as Alaska, what would it not have given for a territory adjacent to its own growing states, and required as a field for the irrepressible energies of its fast increasing population. If that Government considered Alaska worth seven millions of dollars to it, it is not hazarding much to say that, it would have considered the Hudson's Bay Company Territory better worth seventy millions. It is manifest from the foregoing statements that no analogy or common ground exists upon which a comparison between the amount mentioned in the negotiations, and the value of the present claims, is possible. But it may, nevertheless, be easily shewn that the arrangement proposed by the Hudson's Bay Company, or even that finally dictated by the Imperial Government and accepted, involves, prospectively, a very large amount, and may come up to a sum which, with the attendant advantages of the arrangement, would render it not an unprofitable one to the Company.

It is to be observed that the last offer of the Company, made the 13th May, 1868, was to accept £1,000,000 sterling with one-tenth of the land, exclusive of tracts of from 6,000 to 3,000 acres around each post, and certain exemptions from taxation of great value.— (Lord Kimberley's Letter, p. 145, and Sir Stafford Northcote, 13th May, 1868, p. 176.) This was after a correspondence of many years, dating from as far back as 1863. That offer, therefore, is to be taken as the *minimum* for which the Company felt willing, even under the circumstances adverted to, to cede its rights to the Crown.

Then followed a short correspondence and the paper from the Canadian Delegates addressed to Sir Frederick Rogers, February 8th, 1869. (p. 191. special passages, p. 210-11-12-14-21). Of that paper it need only be said that it virtually denies all the rights of the Company. As to the calculation in it based upon the amount of assets, furnished in the prospectus upon the re-organization of the business of the Hudson's Bay Company in 1863, the subject of that prospectus and the argument of the Respondents upon it, are fully disposed of in the pages 27, 28, 29 of the closing argument of the Claimants in reply to the responsive argument of the Uni d States.

There is one letter subsequently from Sir Stafford Northcote, and after the interval of a few days the letter from the Colonial Office proposed or rather prescribed certain terms, not as a basis for further negotiations but as an *ultimatum* for the settlement of the difficulty, in support of which Her Majesty's Government declared " they would be prepared to use all the influence which they could legitimately exercise."

There are passages in this letter which express so well the amount of pressure upon the Hudson's Bay Company, that it will be well to lay them before the Commissioners.

" It is, in Lord Granville's opinion, of very great importance " that this question should be settled on a permanent footing, and " with little delay. He does not disguise the interest which Her " Majesty's Government have in this settlement. It is not cre- " ditable to this country, that any inhabited part of Her Majesty's " Dominions should be without a recognized Government capable of " enforcing the law, and responsible to neighbouring countries for " the performance of international obligations. The toleration of " such a state of things in parts of the Hudson's Bay Territory is " not without danger to the peaceful relations between this country " and the United States. And this danger and injustice are likely to " increase, in proportion as the Mining and Agricultural capabilities " of what is called the " Fertile Belt," begin to attract settlers " from the East and South."

" To Canada, the settlement of the question is not less important, " as removing a cause of irritation between it and its neighbours, " and even with the mother country itself, as destroying an obstacle " to that which has been looked upon as the natural growth of the " Dominion, as likely to open an indefinite prospect of employment " to Canadian labour and enterprise ; and lastly, as enlarging the " inducements which Canada is able to offer to the British immigrant. " It is no small matter that it would enable Her Majesty's Govern-

" ment at once to annex to the Dominion the whole of British North
" America proper, except the colony of British Columbia. * * *

" After repeated communications with both parties, his Lordship is
" convinced that he will be serving the interests of the Dominion, of
" the Company, and of this country, by laying before the Canadian
" Representatives and the Directors of the Company a distinct pro-
" posal, which, as it appears to be, it is for the interest of both par-
" ties to accept, and in support of which Her Majesty's Govern-
" ment would be prepared to use all the influence which they could
" legitimately exercise. ·

" If the proposal is really an impartial one, Lord Granville
" cannot expect that it will be otherwise than unacceptable to both
" of the parties concerned. But he is not without hope that both
" may find, on consideration, that, if it does not give them all that
" they conceive to be their due, it secures to them what is politic-
" ally or commercially necessary, and places them at once in a
" position of greater advantage with reference to their peculiar ob-
" jects than that which they at present occupy. * * * * *

" It is due both to the representatives of Canada and to the
" Company to add that these terms are not intended by Lord
" Granville as the basis of further negotiation, but a final effort to
" effect that amicable accommodation of which he has almost des-
" paired, but which he believes will be for the ultimate interest
" of all parties."

The articles of the proposal, 12 in number, are omitted as they
have already been put of record by the Counsel for the United
States.

Having thus cursorily adverted to this correspondence, I have
but a word to say on the terms prescribed. The only element in
the offer certainly appreciable in money is the £300,000. It is
difficult to say what may be the precise value of the other compensation given; but it cannot be regarded as inconsiderable.

1. The Company is to be relieved of heavy burdens in the main-
tenance of a local government and courts of justice, and of other
institutions in its territory.

2. The country is to be colonized. A constitutional form of
government is to be established, roads and other facilities for
intercourse are to be constructed, telegraph lines completed and

all the operations and aids necessary to the civilization, and the population of the territory are to be carried out at the public expense.

3. One twentieth of the land, exclusive of 50,000 acres around its posts, is to remain in the possession of the Company, and its trade is to be continued without hindrance.

The prospective advantages of this arrangement must be very great. What they may amount to, within 50 years when the country is filled with an industrious and thriving people, and its resources become fully developed, it is impossible to say, but the Company must at all events profit every year from the increase in value of the land reserved to it (which will amount to many millions of acres) by means which will cost it nothing; while the escape from actual burdens, the benefit of a constitutional government, of being part of a young and prosperous Confederation, and having a common interest with the whole of British America, and the growth of its trade turned into new channels corresponding with the growth and changed circumstances of the country, promise advantages which cannot now be estimated, but which all shew how unreasonable it is to attempt to find in the terms of this transfer any standard of value of the claims now before the Commission. If any sound comparison could really be made the Claimants would have no reason to fear the result.

The view taken of the true value of the Company's Territory, actual and prospective, may be found in a pamphlet published in London in 1866, entitled: "A Million, shall we take it."

But I will not prolong this paper, for I am perfectly confident that the Honorable the Commissioners, will not find in these negotiations, or in the acceptance by the Company of the terms prescribed by Her Majesty's Government, anything which affords a basis of comparison as to value between the Territory ceded and the Claims now before them; and still less will they admit any imperfect analogy to affect the direct, positive and overwhelming proof of value which the Claimants have put of record.

The last paragraph in the observations of the learned Counsel for the United States, refers to several positions assumed by him in his Responsive argument. These have all been specially treated and successfully disposed of in the Reply for the Claimants. It may however, be noticed that the connection in which he places the words "*Land or other property lawfully acquired*" is erroneous. These words do not apply to the Hudson's Bay Company, whose possessory, rights without qualification or limitation, are to be respected, but they apply to all British subjects (other than the Company,) These must have been already in the occupation of land or other property to fall within the terms of the 3rd Article of the Treaty. That this is the true meaning, is shown by the context and the division of the sentence by punctuation. This proper reading is of importance, because it involves a recognition of the titles given by the Hudson's Bay Company to its servants as is shown on pages 23 and 24 of the opening argument, and to the Puget Sound Agricultural Company, but it is not material to the case in any other point of view.

I abstain from further observation, respectfully submitting that nothing has been produced which can be accepted as in the least degree impairing the Claimants' evidence, of record anterior to the 23rd of February last or as otherwise affecting their claim.

(Signed)   CHAS. D. DAY,
Counsel for H. B. Co.

www.ingramcontent.com/pod-product-compliance
Lightning Source LLC
Chambersburg PA
CBHW032116080426
42733CB00008B/963